Tony Husband was born thirty-seven years ago and is married to Carole, with a son, Paul. He lives in the North on the edge of the countryside.

He was joke cartoonist of the year for 1984 and 1985 and strip cartoonist of the year for 1987 for 'Yobs' in *Private Eye*.

He is a regular contributor to *Private Eye*, *Punch*, *Playboy*, and many other magazines. He has had a number of books published and co-edits *Oink!* comic which he also co-founded.

THE GREATEST STORY NEVER TOLD

CARTOONS BY TONY HUSBAND
WITH A FOREWORD BY TERRY JONES

CORGI

THE GREATEST STORY NEVER TOLD

A CORGI BOOK 0 552 13340 X

First publication in Great Britain

Corgi edition published 1988

Corgi Books are published by Transworld Publishers Ltd., 61-63 Uxbridge Road, Ealing, London W5 5SA, in Australia by Transworld Publishers (Australia) Pty. Ltd., 15-23 Helles Avenue, Moorebank, NSW 2170, and in New Zealand by Transworld Publishers (N.Z.) Ltd., Cnr. Moselle and Waipareira Avenues, Henderson, Auckland.

Reproduced, printed and bound in Great Britain by
Hazell Watson & Viney Limited
Member of BPCC plc
Aylesbury, Bucks

For
Jim, Keith and Ronnie
(nearly three wise men)

Foreword

I have always thought that the Bible was far too good and resilient a book to be restricted to those interpreters who only want to turn it into long commercials for talking very quietly and looking into the middle distance with shining eyes.

Tony Husband re-interprets the Good Book with a cartoonist's eye, and in so doing, he hits upon moments of truth as well as moments of real humour.

Such an endeavour can only widen the appeal of the original, and help Tony pay-off the instalments on his new vacuum cleaner. I wish him the best of luck with it, and hope that he will continue to enjoy many hours of hoovering in the future.

Terry Jones
8th February 1988

IN THE JUST BEFORE THE BEGINNING

'Tum Te Tum Te Tum.'

'Tum Te Tum Tum Te Tum.'

'Let there be light.'

'Well, what doth thou thinkest?'

'I know! Let's get someone famous to open it'

'You must be joking!'

'I wonder if that's the tree?'

THE END IS NIGH

'That's no problem. I looked bloody silly with legs anyway.'

DO YOU FEEL ALLRIGHT ABEL? YOU DON'T LOOK WELL
NEVER FELT GETTER, LORD

'Build an ark, you? You can't even put up a set of shelves!'

FASTER!
COME ON!
MOVE IT!

'Elephant overboard!'

'Shrew overboard!'

ARK

'No, you can't play with Isaac. His dad's gone to sacrifice him on the mountain.'

'Oh, thank you God! ... Thank you very much!'

'Joseph! Phew! For a minute I thought it was Dr. Who.'

'A plague of frogs in the north will move slowly south, replaced over the weekend by a plague of locusts. The outlook for ...'

'Frogs and locusts I don't mind, but this plague of twentieth century pop-up toasters ...'

HALT
CHOSEN PEOPLE
CROSSING

'Take ten? ... What, any ten?'

'½ dozen eggs, bread, raisins ... Oh! Sorry, that's my shopping list.'

'... Thou shalt not covet thy neighbour's wife ...'

'Oi, Moses! How about throwing in "Thou shalt not make smelly trumps"?'

'Thou shalt not worship these graven images.'

'A One, A Two, A One, Two, Three, Four!'

'Idiot! I said shave his hair off—not re-style it!'

I ♥ GOLIATH
I ♥ GOLIATH
I ♥ GOLIATH

'Bad luck that: killing the giant, then it falling on him.'

'Clear off! We're begatting!'

ELIJAH ON THE MOUNT

DANIEL IN THE LIONS DEN

'... or was it seven fat cows ate seven
... No, there were some cows, er ...
seven thin ones ... I think ... That's it!
Seven ... er ... hang about ...'

Dear Diary,
It's been one of those days: sheep rustled, cattle destroyed, lost all my children, and now I've come out in boils ...

'Er, Mr. Meshack, do you do anything else besides walk through fire?'

'Come on! You can't all be the first born.'

'Now, let's get this right: your house was destroyed by fire and brimstone. Your wife turned into a pillar of salt. Yes, go on ...'

A STAR IS BORN

'There! At last we have found it.'

'All right then, Jesus! But I still prefer Neville.'

'Sod them! Where's the gold, incense and myrrh?'

'All right Salome, you can have his head – just stop dancing.'

TRAVEL AGENTS
40 DAYS IN THE WILDERNESS EXCLUSIVE
UNDER 30s GETAWAY
DEAD SEA FUN + FROLICS

'He's coming! He's coming!'

DING DONG
DING
CHOC ICE
CORNET
MR SOPPY
ICES + LOLLIES

NEWS
MAN
WALKS
ON WATER
SENSATION

MIND YOUR HALO

'Well, to be quite honest, they're not the twelve I'd have picked.'

KICK ME

'O.K. Lazarus, come on out! We know you're in there!'

'Thank God! Super Samaritan.'

'Here Lord! How to feed 5,000 with a few fish and a bit of bread.'

'My son's named his pet hamster after you.'

MEANWHILE
ELSEWHERE

HOSANA!
HOSANA!
GIFTS and SOU
I ♥ JC
JESUS PENCILS
JESUS WALK ON WATER BOOTS

'Table for thirteen! Have you booked?'

'So that's eight soups, 4 prawn cocktail, one pate starter. Five steaks well done, two ...'

'When you say "Last Supper", you actually mean your last supper, not our's, don't you?'

'Tonight, one of you will betray me.'

BARABUS! BARABUS! BARABUS!

'Typical, you wait ages for one and three come together.'

'Yes, surely he is the son of … er …
what's his name?'

'Well, he was there five minutes ago.'

PUNCH +JUDAS

PAUL BLINDED BY THE LIGHT ON THE ROAD TO DAMASCUS

ST PAUL WAS
BLINDED
BY THE LIGHT
HERE

FIRE
Je suis
Danken Schön
BASTA!
BASTA!
HASTA LA VISTA

BOOKSHOP
BIBLE SIGNING TODAY